YOU'RE ALL YOU NEED

Real Happiness Through The Power of Meditation

Sarah Rowland

Copyright © 2016 by Sarah Rowland

All rights reserved. No part of this book may be reproduced or transmitted in any form or by any means, electronic or mechanical, including photocopying, recording or by any information storage and retrieval system without written permission of the publisher, except for the inclusion of brief quotations in a review.

TABLE OF CONTENTS

INTRODUCTION 1

Chapter 1 *What Is Meditation?* 2

Chapter 2 *43 Spectacular Benefits Of Meditation* 9

Chapter 3 *Types Of Meditation – Pick The One That Works For You.* 15

Chapter 4 *The 5-Minute Meditation* 25

Chapter 5 *10 Minute Guided Meditation Techniques* 28

Chapter 6 *The Fifteen Minute Anxiety Killing And Confidence Building Guided Meditation* 44

Chapter 7 *The Twenty Minute Body Scan* 58

Chapter 8 *The 25 Minute Blissful Mind Meditation* 68

Chapter 9 *The 30-Minute Meditation* 83

Conclusion 104

INTRODUCTION

Congratulations on downloading this book and thank you for doing so.

The following chapters will discuss Meditation and the various ways to practice Meditation in your life.

There are plenty of books on this subject on the market, thanks again for choosing this one! Every effort was made to ensure it is full of as much useful information as possible, please enjoy!

CHAPTER 1

What Is Meditation?

Ask anyone around you what meditation is and they'll most likely come with answers such as it is a prayer or some form of worship or mental concentration. If meditation can be powerfully summed up in a few words – it is a way of life. Meditation is absolute awareness of the present. Anything you do with keen awareness and focus is meditation. Mindful walking or concentrating on your breath can also be meditation. Listening to the sound of hustling trees, a gushing waterfall or birds chirping in your backyard is also meditation. When you direct you consciousness to any activity or object around you without any distraction, you are practicing meditation.

Contrary to popular misconception, meditation is not a method but simply a way of life. Meditation is a lifestyle. It is a state of being when the mind is liberated from all its chaotic thoughts to focus on the present. It is nourishment for your soul. It celebrates universal value such as kindness, sharing, nonviolence, peace, responsibility and more. In an era where humanity and the world around us is quickly fragmenting, meditation guides us towards a peaceful path.

The term is used inaccurately and freely in the contemporary world, which is why there is a sense of ambiguity associated with it. Some people use the term meditation for contemplation or the process of thinking. Others go a step further and think meditation is all about day dreaming or visually fantasizing. Meditation can be any of these. However at its core, it is attaining a restful mind. Meditation is not religion. It is a spiritual science that encapsulates discipline, well-defined principles and verifiable results.

To reach the perfect state of meditation, we require focus instead of a scattered mind and clarity in place of dullness. There has to be an increasing keenness to observe our thoughts and state of mind instead of being clouded by emotions or prejudice. Meditation will train you to be honest to yourself rather than playing deception games and walking free from unpleasant problems. You need endless reserves of patience since you won"t become an overnight Zen master. Operating from a level of self-acceptance, self-assuredness, confidence, energy and enthusiasm brings more peace to the mind. Balance and harmony are the most popular meditation buzzwords. It is all about achieving a state of balance or harmony with your physical, mental and spiritual faculties.

A Tibetan Lama was closely monitored by a brain scan machine to examine physiological functions during a deep state of meditation. The scientist helming the experiment said, "Very well Sir. The machine reveals that your brain can slip into a deep state of relaxation. It validates your practice." "No", replied the Lama, pointing to his brain, "This validates your machine."

The word meditation originates from two Latin terms: mediatari (which means to think or dwell upon) and mederi (which means to heal). The Sanskrit derivative „medha" implies wisdom.

Meditation is a wonderful means or transforming the body, mind and spirit. A disciplined and consistent meditation practice has several benefits, including enhanced concentration, calmness, positivity and clarity. Meditation has the ability to transform your thought patterns and mental habits to cultivate a newer and more positive way of being. With dedicated practice, you nurture a profoundly serene and energized mind state. These experiences have a completely transformational effect, and can lead to a newer level of understanding lie.

The basic objective of meditation is spiritual renewal and to achieve a state of absolute peace. Meditation helps expand the practitioner"s realm of conscious to enable them to let go of the physiological rigidity of attachments. You learn to move above the pettiness of ego, insecurity, vanity and snobbery. There is a greater sense of elevation and unison with a strong spiritual force that endows us with emotional maturity.

The history of meditative practice is closely interwoven into a religious context within cultures that subscribed to its philosophy. Some of the most ancient meditation references can be traced back to the Vedas of Hindu religion prevalent in India and Nepal. Around 6th or 5th centuries BCE, other types of meditation such as Confucianism and Taoism evolved in China, in addition to a variety of practices that developed in Hinduism, Buddhism and Jainism in India and Nepal.

In the west the seed of meditation was planted in 20 BCE, when Philo of Alexandria wrote about some kind of spiritual exercises marked by concentration and attention. Plotinus took the theory further in the 3rd century to develop full-fledged meditation techniques.

There are a staggering variety of meditation techniques since the practice is highly personal. Some practices such as mindful meditation and focused attention are heavily rooted in scientific research. The focus can be on anything from breathing to a bodily sensation to a specific external object. One of the core aspects of meditation is to singularly focus on a single point or objects, and draw attention to this focal point when the mind starts wandering.

Meditation harbors several misunderstandings, including the notion that one must cease to think while meditating. While silencing the distracting noise originating in the mind is valid, there"s no way you can stop thinking completely. The objective is not to stop thinking but cultivation of clearer insights by drowning out the pointless noise that stems from within, using discrimination. You don"t need to stop thinking. You only need to halt compulsive, robotic, unintelligent mental activities that induce fatigue, are generally pointless and sometimes, downright dangerous.

Ajahn Chah, an influential Buddhadhamma teacher said, ""Try to be mindful, and let things take their natural course. Then your mind will become still in any surroundings, like a clear forest pool. All kinds of wonderful, rare animals will come to drink at the pool, and you will clearly see the nature of all things. But you will be still. This is the happiness of the Buddha."

Meditation is actually a three way process that that involves a powerful state of consciousness brining clarity, calmness and bliss. The first step is about receiving sensory stimuli and reacting in more uncontrolled manner. It is about bouncing from thought to thought by following different physical and psychological reactions. The same thought or stimulus can bring about different reactions at various times. For example, we may spot a dog and feel nostalgic about a cute pet we once had and loved. It triggers a comforting and warm feeling in us, where we achieve a state of relaxation. In a different situation we may start fearing the dog, thinking it may start attacking us and develop thoughts of paranoia, feeling more fearful and physically rigid.

It is commonly accepted fact that focusing your thinking on a single behavior can transform your habits. For instance, athletes who constantly visualize playing successfully end up advancing their game considerably. Meditation is also about saying and doing things that drive our subconscious mind towards your goals. It can be harnessed in multiple ways provided you have the power to recognize its benefits.

CHAPTER 2

43 Spectacular Benefits Of Meditation

We all know by now that meditation is good for us. How exactly though? There have been innumerable studies and extensive research projects to explore the impact of meditation in everyday life. Want some reasons to kick-start a solid meditation practice. We take you through the powerful benefits of a dedicated, consistent and disciplined meditation lifestyle.

1. Meditation enhances the flow of air into our lungs, thus making breathing easier.
2. It lowers your heart rate and boosts blood flow within the body.
3. Meditation reduces chronic illnesses such as arthritis and allergies.
4. A regular and consistent meditation practice improves your overall immunity.
5. Meditation assists in weight loss.
6. It prolongs the process of aging to give you a fresher, more youthful and rejuvenated appearance.

7. Meditation is highly effective for combating headaches and migraine.
8. It boosts your athletic performance.
9. Meditation is great for fighting stress induced infertility.
10. It builds high levels of self confidence and self esteem.
11. Meditation enhances creativity and productivity.
12. It increases the practitioner's ability to solve complicated problems.
13. Meditation awards the practitioner with greater emotional stability.
14. It gives you the vision to see the larger perspective in any situation.
15. Meditation enhances your memory power and learning abilities.
16. Meditation increases self-awareness, acceptance and happiness.
17. A regular meditation practice reduces depression and other mental ailments.

18. Meditation reduces pre and post partum depression in women.

19. It boosts the concentration of the brain's grey matter, thus enhancing our cognitive abilities.

20. Meditation helps you live in the present and develop a deep sense of gratitude and appreciation for it.

21. It helps in quitting smoking, alcohol and other addictions.

22. Meditation helps you sleep better

23. It reduces your aggression level.

24. A regular meditation practice diminishes anxiety and restless thoughts.

25. Meditation helps in making sounder decisions and more accurate judgments.

26. It awards you the calmness to act in productive and considerate manner.

27. Reduces dependency on pills and drugs.

28. Meditation helps you develop a higher sense of intuition.

29. It assists in creating sexual desire and energy.

30. Meditation is an excellent way for curing phobias and deep seated fears.

31. It facilitates better communication between the brain"s left and right hemisphere.

32. Meditation helps you experiences a profound sense of assurance.

33. Regular meditation practitioners experience a lesser need for medical care.

34. Meditation helps decrease muscle tension.

35. A consistent and disciplined meditation practice is wonderful for developing will-power.

36. Meditation offers a greater sense of inner-directedness.

37. It increases compassion and empathy for other beings.

38. A consistent meditation practice lowers cholesterol levels, thus lowering the risk of heart diseases.

39. Meditation provides substantial relief to asthma patients.

40. It keeps the body"s hormones well balanced to award practitioners a more radiant and beautiful skin.

41. Meditation acts as a effective recovery mechanism for food related addiction such as binge eating.

42. Meditation enhances your sense of focus and concentration.

43. Meditation is excellent for countering grief after the loss of a loved one.

CHAPTER 3

Types Of Meditation – Pick The One That Works For You.

Straight off, there's no good, bad, better or „more effective than the other" meditation technique. There are several techniques and all are wonderful, depending on what exactly you are seeking though a meditative practice. For instance, if you are looking for a more stress-free that comprises living in the present than worrying about the future, mindful meditation can work wonders. Similarly, if your idea is to fulfill a goal through meditation, visualization can be a highly potent technique. We bring you a treasure trove of different types of meditation to help you decide the one that works best for you.

Guided Visualization – Guided visualization is a relatively new technique that aims to offer enhanced personal development and goal achievement. The premise on which it is based is, "we become what we think." The focus is on setting clear goals and meditating while visualizing the goal in order to fulfill it. Practitioners visualize their goal in a relaxed and positive manner by imagining themselves in a desirable situation. A guide or master conducts the entire meditation through the process of a powerful narration that takes you through circumstances that you wish to manifest through the process.

Beginners commence their guided visualization practice with an instructor

Mindfulness – Mindful meditation is another popular meditation form that hails from the Buddhist tradition. This technique is all about being fully immersed in your present, and observing your thoughts in a non-judgmental manner. It is acknowledging the present, allowing the mind to stray, accepting any thoughts that arise, and being fully aware of the present. The practice comprises sitting crossed legged and focusing attention completely on the breath. When wandering thoughts take over, the practitioner simply acknowledges them, and gently returns focus back to the breath or object. Research has strongly pointed out to the fact that a disciplined and consistent mindfulness practice reduces stress, overcomes depression and combats distress.

In the east, mindful meditation is often referred to as Vipassana. The term Vipassana translates into "insight or wisdom into reality" and that is precisely why it is also referred to as "insight meditation." This is one of the most ancient meditation practices that goes back to the 6th century BC.

Like other meditation techniques, there"s no right or ideal way to practice Vipassana or mindful meditation. A majority of practitioners start with mindful breathing or observing the breath in a judgment free manner. The practice then graduates to mindfully observing bodily sensations or thought patterns.

Qi Gong – Qi Gong is one of the oldest forms of Chinese meditation for boosting posture, respiration and relaxation. This meditation technique comprises using your breath to pass on energy throughout the body along with its core energy centers. There is a greater focus on movement and relaxing breathing methods. Qi Gong is excellent for reducing stress and stress induced conditions.

Transcendental – Transcendental meditation was founded by Maharishi Mahesh Yogi, and involves the use of a series of mantras for focusing and following one"s breath. The mantra differs according to a large number of factors, including the practitioner"s birth year or gender. Transcendental meditation is practiced by being in a seated position.

Movement Meditation – Movement meditation can be challenging for newbies, given the fact that it can be highly soothing and energizing all the same. The technique involves being seated and keeping your eyes closed, while concentrating on your breath, and trying out various flowing movements repetitively. Simply turn focus on the movement instead of a sound or thought or physical sensation. This can also be therapeutic for the body, and can boost circulation.

Reflective Meditation – Reflective meditation comprises reflecting upon a question, problem, topic or theme that requires contemplation or analysis. Practitioners gently draw the mind to a focused topic when it wanders. Conventionally, reflective meditation is used for gaining insight into the real meaning of perplexing concepts such as life, relationships, death, conscience and much more.

There are many professional or personal challenges we face in our day to day life, the conclusive insights to which lie in ancient philosophy and religious scriptures. Through contemplative and introspective meditation, we gain the needed wisdom and insights, which in turn leads to greater conviction. Practitioners will often be surprised at the breakthrough or innovative solutions they come up with through reflection or reflective meditation. This form of meditation is also valuable in understanding inner conflict issues that can come up as a result of a meditation practice.

Affirmation Meditation – Affirmation meditation is a technique that uses affirmations or positive thoughts as a way to firmly embed specific thoughts into the subconscious mind with the intention of manifesting these thoughts. The technique involves getting into a relaxed state, which makes the practitioner more suggestive. This helps the brain receive the message in more effective manner to influence your actions in the direction of the affirmation. Affirmations can involve physical health, focus, confidence, abundance, magnetism and much more.

Metta Meditation or Loving Kindness – This type of meditation comprises nurturing unconditional kindness and love for other living beings. Since kindness and empathy is the basis of Metta meditation, it is also referred to as compassion meditation. Research has suggested that a regular practice of Metta meditation leads to greater happiness, increased brain wave activity and balanced behavior.

Metta is love without any attachment and the objective is to boost a sense of harmony and goodwill for others. The practice starts with complete acceptance and unconditional love for oneself. The idea is to fully accept and love yourself before you can begin to love others unconditionally. This may not be one of the most popular meditation techniques but it can be equally effective when it comes to improving your mood and interpersonal relationships.

When practiced regularly, this form of mediation leads to absolute joy. This type of meditation is brilliant for practitioners suffering from negative thoughts, anger, aggression and depression. It is not possible to feel loving kindness and aggression at the same time. Metta meditation triggers your brain"s happiness centers.

Mantra Meditation – Mantra meditation is ideal for people who find serenity in repeating a positive mantra. It involves a single repetitive sound or bunch of sounds to empty the mind. By reciting a mantra or rhythmic song, the mind learns to release stress and develop keen focus. Mantras can either be sung loudly or repeated silently. A simple, effective yet powerful onomatopoeia is Ohm. The practice is ideal for beginners keen on maintaining a serious, disciplined and focused meditation practice.

Heart Centered Meditation – Heart centered is carried out to release negative energies, fears and grief. Its main objective is to heal the heart. The technique focuses on feeling a sense of connectedness with your heart and those of others. This meditation practice is especially useful for those suffering from a loss or grieving. It helps heal the heart and ease the pain of suffering.

Kundalini Meditation - The core philosophy of Kundalini meditation involves awakening the body"s dormant Kundalini energy (located at the end of your spine) through the power of meditation. Kunalini awakening is nothing but directing the energy up the spine, which is eventually believed to lead to an enlightened state. Kundalini meditation comprises a combination of breathing technique, hand placements (mudras) and chants (mantras). These tap into subconscious mind, and lead it to awaken, stimulate and energize the conscious mind. Open minded practitioners looking to explore their spirituality.

Chakra Meditation – Chakras are seven energy centers located in different regions of the body. Each of them is associated with a distinct sound, energy characteristic and color. Chakra meditations can be brilliantly combined with a yogic practice. The emphasis is on focusing on any physical or psychological aspect. Chakras meditations again use a combination of meditation techniques such as visualization, mudras and sound to heal a compelling emotional issue. Chakra meditations work well for those who are already practicing yoga, those looking to heal from an emotional or physical condition through energy and spiritually inclined practitioners.

Tonglen Meditation – Tonglen meditation is a Tibetian Buddhist discipline that is created for helping a practitioner connect with their suffering with the intention of helping them overcome it. The discipline"s premise is a total antithesis to the philosophy of the western world that subscribes to pleasure as a means of avoiding pain. Toglen trains you to manage suffering, pain and life"s challenges. It helps you develop a sense of openness and acceptance for pain. It helps you release negativity, practice give and take, and nurture a sense of compassion through breathing, visualization techniques and powerful intention. Anyone dealing with stress, negativity, self doubt and difficult people can explore the benefits of Tonglen meditation.

CHAPTER 4

The 5-Minute Meditation

Duration – 5 minutes

Objective – To De-stress, Relax and Focus. These can also be used as warm ups for the more lengthier and intense meditation sessions described later in the book.

Setting – Begin by sitting in comfortable position. Use props such as cushions to seat yourself in a relaxed and comfortable posture. Practice in a serene and distraction free environment. Use aroma candles, incense or essential oils if required to create a soothing and energized setting.

Begin – Close your eyes.

Relax completely. Release all the tension from your body.

Spend a few minutes to gather yourself into the moment.

Let the breathing flow

Breathe in to the count of 1- 4 as your lungs expand

Breathe out to the count of 1-4 as your lungs contract

Allow each body muscle to relax as you breathe.

Let every ounce of stress fade away.

With each breathe out, exhale any leftover stress, worries and tension of the day

Allow yourself to relax completely

While breathing, imagine being on a lovely beach, while experiencing its warm, soothing and relaxing waves.

It is forming right at your toes with each deep breath you take.

The wave is slowly moving upwards.

It touches your feet first and slowly moves to your legs.

The wave then gradually touches your stomach and chest.

It moves to your arms, and finally above your head, relaxing and calming your body completely as your breathe. Your body is now completely free from any stress, tension or rigidity.

CHAPTER 5

10 Minute Guided Meditation Techniques

Meditation 1

Duration: 10 Minutes

Objective: To De-Stress, Relax, Concentrate and Sleep Better

We all know the mind can be exceedingly noisy. There"s so much chaos and clutter occupying our mind all the time. Most people believe that meditation isn"t suitable for them because they can"t halt their thoughts. However, this is the exact objective of meditation. Meditation is all about watching your thoughts come, evolve and go. It is about keenly tuning in to the thoughts. What we are doing is strengthening the attention muscle. Every time we recognize a thought and gently draw our focus back, we are building that vital attention/focus muscle. Think of meditation as a paper folding exercise. It takes focus, effort and diligence to get it right the first time around. However with time and practice, the act becomes seamless. Be gentle with yourself.

Forcing yourself to meditate can be highly counterproductive. Treat the practice with some humor, kindness and curiosity. A popular meme doing rounds on the social media fittingly sums up the new age attitude towards mediation. It goes, "come on inner peace, I don"t have all day." Don"t try to force or induce peace into your being. Let it come gradually, naturally and soothingly.

Here"s a 10 minute guided meditation you"re absolutely going to love.

Find a comfortable seating position. Close your eyes when you are ready.

Pay close attention to your thoughts.

Notice the thoughts that pop into the head.

Are you thinking about what tasks need to done during the day or what just happened before you started meditating?

Simply notice your thoughts.

Take 3 cleansing breaths by inhaling through the nose and exhaling through your mouth.

Feel the breath completely and deep into your body.

Breathe into your chest and stomach.

Breathe into your ribs and back.

Each time the mind wanders, simply return to the breathing sensation and notice your breathing pattern. You mind will stray. It is natural. Bring it back gently into the physical sensations felt while breathing. Feel the wonderful air around you touching the tip of your nose. Notice how the air fills up your lungs.

Take the time to tune in to your environment

Closely notice the sounds surrounding you. What do you hear? The ventilation system hum? Sounds from the adjoining street? Birds chirping in your backyard? Gradually, start noticing the smallest sounds, including the sound of your breath.

Feel a sense of unison with the environment and yourself.

Be fully present. Catch yourself noticing thoughts.

Begin notice the things around you keenly. Start with the chair or seat on which your have positioned yourself.

Then, move on to the floor touching your feet.

Feel the air that touches your skin.

Start scanning your physical body.

Again, when you begin noticing thoughts occupying your mind, simply go back to the scanning process.

Start with your soles. Move up to the feet, calves, legs and thighs. Do not skip the joints. Do not simply think about the various body parts while scanning but actually feel them. Try and tune into the feeling each part induces. Notice is you experience any compelling emotions within the body. Do you feel any tension or soreness within the back, shoulders, joints and muscles? Do you notice any wandering thoughts? Simply pick up from where you left off.

Keep inhaling and repeat a mantra such as "breathe in", and exhale with "breathe out." Make it easy, natural and effortless. Each time your mind strays, get it back with the mantra, "breathe in" and "breathe out." Keep breathing in and out while repeating the mantra for a few seconds. Allow your mind to be free to expand its awareness. Think of this as watching a movie or listening to a song. How far can it really go? Its zoom out time.

Draw the awareness back to your body.

Keenly feel the chair you are sitting on.

Notice the air temperature against your skin.

Watch out sounds that you haven"t bothered about until now.

When you are done, open your eyes.

Notice where your thoughts are heading.

Are you excited about the task that"s coming up or are you able to experience a sense of stillness in the present?

Meditation 2

Duration: 10 Minutes

Objective: To De-Stress, Relax and Focus

Find a comfortable seating position and close your eyes once you are all set.

Let your mouth and jaw relax effortlessly. Find the perfect position. Do not clench it too tight or keep it wide open.

Begin with deep, soothing and relaxing breaths.

Breathe in through the nose and breathe out through the mouth.

Fill your lungs and stomach with the air through every breath.

Empty it through each exhalation.

Practice this multiple times.

Now get back to your natural breathing pattern.

Inhale and exhale through the nose. The breathing should be your normal breathing, easy and effortless. Let go of the urge to control the breath"'s rhythm.

Continue breathing. Tune in to what is happening inside and around you.

Keep your ears open for different sounds.

Feel the chair you are sitting on.

Feel the skin of your feet touch the ground.

Just like the previous meditation, begin scanning your body. Start from your feet and move right up to the crown of the head. Take a few minutes to do this. Closely feel any sensations that originate. Draw awareness to different body parts as they you go on scanning upwards. Feel sensations without naming or labeling them as positive or negative.

Each time your mind wanders, gently carry it back to the sensations. Take some time out to reflect upon our mood. How do you feel today? Tune into any compelling emotions you are currently experiencing. Can you pinpoint the exact location where these emotions are housed? Is it your stomach or chest or head? Emotions can accumulate in several places within the body.

Concentrate on your breath now.

Start repeating the "breathe in" and "breathe out" mantra, while following your natural breathing pattern. Say "breathe in" each time you inhale and "breathe out" every time you exhale. Keep repeating the mantra, while keeping your attention firmly fixated on the tip of your nose.

Each time, you find your focus being challenged; simply get back to the breathing and mantra. Breathe in and breathe out. Recognize your drifting thoughts, and gently bring it back. Have you ever trained a puppy or witnessed one being trained? You have to guiding it back each time it wanders, with love, compassion and patience. Thoughts experienced during meditation are similar to training a puppy. They have to diverted to the point of focus with loving kindness and patience.

Breathe in and breathe out using the mantra.

Now breathe naturally without the mantra.

Now, set your mind free, expanding the realm of your attention as far as possible. Become completely aware of your senses. Feel your body weight. Tune in to the sounds engulfing your surroundings. Be aware of your breathing, thoughts and this voice directing you. Can your mind simply take a step back from it all? Be aware of everything without actually being a part of it. Can you view things inside and around you objectively? Can you for a short-while act like a third person who is observing your life in a non-judgmental manner? Can you be the audience watching a movie on your life?

Now slowly come back to your body. Feel your breath. How does your body feel while coming in contact with the seat or chair? How does it feel when your feet touch the ground? Notice the sounds surrounding you. Enjoy an intense, deep and cleansing breath. Breathe in and out loudly. Tune in to the sound of your breath. Gradually open your eyes.

Meditation 3

The Smile and Stay Positive Meditation

Duration – 10 Minutes

Objective – To Stay Happy, Smiling and Positive.

Begin by finding a really comfortable and relaxing place to sit in. Wear comfortable clothes that keep you distraction free and at ease. Sit upright and be as comfortable as possible. Shut your eyes and draw attention to the breath. We begin by practicing deep breathing to calm your senses as your body and mind gradually relax. Inhale to the count of 1-4. Hold your breath at the last count. Breathe out at the count of 1-4.

Draw all the attention to the face. Is there any stress held in your jaw? Is the region behind your eyes, jaw and forehead feeling tensed? Let these regions relax and slow down. Let the cheeks relax completely. There"s no room for any stress or tension on your face. Your cheeks are gradually beginning to form a lovely smile.

Think of something really funny or amusing that happened in the past week. Think about your love for your near and dear ones. Think about all the numerous gifts you"ve been blessed with – a roof above your head, a hot cup of coffee to keep you warm in winters, warm and nutritious meals, the five senses with which you are able to experience the world around you.

You have a pair of footwear to keep your feet protected and clothes to keep you warm. There"s so much to be grateful for in the world around you.

Focus on memories that make you happy. Think about a family reunion or a much awaited Thanksgiving/ Christmas meal. How does it feel to be surrounded by your loved ones? Focus on feelings, memories and instances that evoke a sense of happiness, joy and positivity in you.

If you feel tension accumulating within any part of the body, allow your smile to fix it gradually. Let the smile gently soften the region that is feeling stress and pain. Let the muscles soothe and relax. Stay here for a few seconds until you feel a complete sense of facial relaxation.

Next, move to the other body area that feels tensed, stressed and tight. Infuse a positive, inspiring and spirited smile into your sore muscles. As you infuse smile energy into them, feel the tiredness and soreness fading away. When you smile into stressed muscles, the tension is released. Allow the muscles to completely relax.

Draw awareness into the heart. Experience the heart feeling the warmth and calmness of your smile. Doesn"t your heart brim with happiness? Visualize a circle of love in the heart. As you smile into it, the circle grows. It is now full of pure love energy. The heart is throbbing with this pure, positive and inspiring love energy. The circle grows bigger with every smile you put into it. The love energy is emitting a sparkling pink light. The light represents love and healing. Few things in life are as healing as unconditional love originating from a pure heart. Feel the love and healing coming from your heart. Focus on how your heart feels. Keep this focus for a few seconds. Focus only on the love growing in your heart"s energy circle.

While focusing on the heart, here are some positive affirmations that you can repeat now and throughout the day to brighten up your spirit.

"I am happy, positive and relaxed irrespective of the circumstances."

"The power to remain happy, positive and unaffected lies within me."

"I find it increasingly simple to smile, stay positive and spread happiness."

"I alone am responsible for my well-being and happiness."

"The key to my happiness is in my hands alone."

"Happiness shines easily on me."

"When I am happy, smiling and positive, the whole world is happy with me."

Now, slowly draw awareness to the face again. How do you feel now? Is there a greater feeling of happiness, positivity and lightness? Now, when the session is over, it"ll be simpler for you to smile and stay more positive all through the day. It is time to awaken from the meditative state. Slowly, start brining your body and mind into a state of awareness. When you feel sufficiently ready, gradually start opening your eyes. You are now in a waking consciousness state. Get up and be prepared to spread your joy, happiness, smile, love and positivity all around you.

CHAPTER 6

The Fifteen Minute Anxiety Killing And Confidence Building Guided Meditation

Meditation 1

Duration: 15 minutes

Objective: To overcome anxiety, build confidence and ensure complete relaxation.

The meditation that we are just about to guide you is great for relaxation, combating anxiety and building self-esteem. This one"s great for helping you feel more relaxed, guiding you towards fading your anxieties and helping you clear the mind. Lastly, it helps you find a soothing serenity within the self, where you feel complete safety and calmness.

Make yourself completely comfortable. Sit down in a place that is calm, positively energized and distraction free. You want a place where your worries, stress and problems can melt away.

Let"s begin all you rockstar practitioners.

Shut your eyes, and breathe deeply. Release the breath.

Try and blank out your thoughts. Keep it free from worries. Simply experience stillness and silence. You have a powerful soul. It is stronger than you think. It can guide your body into feeling relaxed and rejuvenated. It has the capacity to heal, nurture, soothe, calm and replenish your spirit. It has the power to mend your broken heart, spirit and confidence. It gives you joy, confidence, glory, happiness and positivity.

Focus on your breath. Notice the oxygen making its way into the nose gradually. Breathe out slowly. When you exhale, concentrate on the pain that"s haunting you. It can be physical or psychological. Know that you are not alone in your suffering.

No harm can come upon you. This is the ideal place to be where your stress, concerns, anxiety and self doubt doesn"t have footholes.

Imagine being on your favorite beach in the world. Feel the soft, flowy and golden sand touching your feet. Feel the gentle, balmy and summery breeze caressing your hair and face. Imagine the warmth of the morning sunshine against your skin. Visualize the images appearing before you. Imagine the ocean"s vastness and infinity. Picture waves crashing against the coast. Immerse into the relaxing and calming sound of the waves. Let it completely fill your mind and relax the body. Feel a growing sense of relaxation beginning to take over your head, neck, shoulders, arms, hands and back. The relaxation is absolutely pure, soothing and intense.

Feel the relaxation slowly enveloping your legs, and then gradually moving to the feet. Your eyes are still shut. Breathe normally. Fill your mind with positivity, gentleness and light. Become aware of your greatness. There is an intensely sparkling light inside your mind, like no one else. Think about the illuminating and incandescent aura you carry around you. There"s no one in the Universe like you. Know that you are capable of achieving much more than you believe with your uniqueness. There is a constant light within you that is leading you towards the greatness you deserve.

Relax now. Get yourself ready to go back to your regular state, filled with a renewed sense of light, positivity and magnificence. Slowly, start gaining awareness of your surroundings. Be prepared to live in peace and harmony not just with yourself but also with your surroundings. Stay still for some time. Enjoy the blissfulness of the place where you are completely and positively yourself.

Take a few deep breaths. Relax. Smile confidently. You are now completely ready to take on the world with your newfound positivity and self-assured smile. The world is waiting to embrace your greatness with open arms. Relax. Slowly open your eyes.

Meditation 2

Loving: Kindness Meditation

Duration: 15 Minutes

This particular exercise draws from the guided meditation put together by researcher Emma Seppala, Director of Science at the Stanford University's Center for Compassion and Altruism Research and Education and the author of The Happiness Track.

Close your eyes slowly. Be seated in comfortable position with your feet placed on the floor and the spine held upright. Relax the entire body. Keep your eyes shut during the entire visualization exercise for more reflective and inward awareness. Do not strain yourself or force yourself to concentrate. Simply relax and follow simple instructions. Take a deep breath in and exhale.

Monitor your breathing pattern as the chest gradually rises. Keep your eyes shut. Think of an individual who is very close to your heart. That person is standing to your right. The person loves you a lot. It could be someone you knew in the past or a person who occupies an important space in your present. The person is standing next to you now, transferring all the love, positivity, assurance and warmth your way from the person. The person wishes you safety, health, happiness, wellness and kindness. Feel the pure love and warmth coming your way.

Visualize another person standing on your left. This is a person who cherishes and loves you deeply. He/she is sending you plenty of wishes for your happiness, wellness and health. Feel a sense of positivity, kindness, warmth and compassion coming your way from this wonderful person.

Now, picture yourself being encircled by all the people you"ve loved dearly in your life and all those who love you or have loved you in the past. Imagine being surrounded by family, friends, loved ones and well-wishers. They are sending you positive wishes and love from everywhere. Your spirit is overflowing with love, positivity, warmth and happiness.

Breathe in slowly. Now breathe out. Relax. Draw your focus back on the individual to your right. Start sending love to the person and experience him/her sending it back to you. You and the person are alike. This individual also seeks happiness like you. Send all the love, warmth, positivity and good wishes to this person.

Draw your awareness back to the person on your left. Start sending love to him/her. Send all the warmth and positivity you can. You and the person are pretty similar to each other. This individual also wishes for happiness, just like you. Send all the love, warmth, positivity and good wishes to this person.

Think of a neutral acquaintance. Someone you haven"t had a chance to know well enough, and who you do not have strong feelings of love or hate for. The only common aspect is that both you and this person desire to lead a good life. Send well-being wishes to this person.

Slowly, expand your awareness and visualize the entire planet. The little globe that holds the entire world is now held in the realm of your mind"s eye. Think of it as a small ball. Send encouraging and positive wishes to every living being on planet earth. They are all like you. Just like you, they wish to be experiences complete happiness.

Take a deep and intense breath. Breathe out. Take another deep breath and let go. Simply notice how your mind feels after the session. Open your eyes slowly once you"re ready.

Meditation 3

Anger and Pain Releasing Meditation

Duration: 15 Minutes

Objective: To release anger and pain held within us.

You many have experienced trauma, violence or mental abuse in your childhood, which may have created a huge reservoir of anger, pain, guilt and resentment within you. You aren"t alone. There are millions of people who have suffered abuse in their childhood, which has had a direct bearing on their thoughts, emotions and actions. This meditation session will help you gradually release pent up anger, and be in a peaceful space. If you feel overwhelmed or overcome by emotions at any stage, simply pause. Practice deep breathing and get back to the session when you feel more mentally ready

for it. You can leave it for a better time if it gets tough. Just do not force yourself to continue when you feel uncomfortable during the meditation process.

Start by taking a few deep and intense breaths. Be completely aware of your breath and you breathe in and out. Inhale slowly. Exhale. Perform this deep breathing exercise for some time till you feel relaxed and more centered. When you inhale, imagine breathing in an incandescent white light into your body. When you breathe out, visualize releasing all the pent up tension, guilt and anger from your body.

Now imagine catching the film of your life in a large and comfortable cinema theatre. The lights have been slowly dimmed. The screen has suddenly lit up to play the movie. Now, it comes alive with a past memory. This is the memory of the thing that caused you intense pain, hurt and anger. Someone from your childhood brought in unpleasant memories of hurt and anger. Now this painful memory is slowly being played on the screen.

See everything you can and try to stay detached from it. View it as an objective audience with no room for attachment or emotions, the way movie critics do when they review films. Look around and see if someone else is present in the theatre. This is the same person from your past who has scarred you. The person is also watching the memory movie play out in front of their eyes.

They are getting slightly uncomfortable, yet cannot escape their past actions.

This person is now getting an account of the pain, hurt and suffering experienced by you as the movie unfolds. The individual is now feeling sad and shedding tears. He/she slowly approaches you and begs your forgiveness. You are in a sort of a complex emotional state yourself, still processing the pain and trauma of the hurtful memory.

Understand that now you are in a completely protected and comfortable space. You are feeling more self-assured, peaceful and empowered. You are in a space where this person slowly ceases to affect you. You are now involved in a conversation with the person who has hurt you. You gently tell them that the past is gone, and that you have forgiven them. You tell them that the hurt they caused you due to their past actions is now a thing of the past that has no relevance to your present or future.

The theatre gradually begins to be filled with a magical violet light. The entire room is engulfed in the magnificence of this radiant violet light. It is as if some magical force has come into being suddenly to take away all your hurt, trauma and pain. Your pain, stress and hurt have evaporated into this shinning violet light. Tears flow from your eyes, but you realize that you are healing at a deeper level. When you inhale, the heart gradually opens. There is deep love, forgiveness and light filling your heart. The love has completely taken over the heart in a surreal, almost magical healing process.

You have now walked ahead and reached over to the person who caused you pain. This person is now held in an embrace by you. Your heart is open now. The multiple layers of anger, suffering, pain and discomfort are evaporating. There is a release and healing

process taking place at a deep level. There is now no guilt, anger, regret, remorse or pain. The feelings may come back as you try to release them. Acknowledge them. Stay with them for as long as it takes to heal you until the negative feelings are completely released. Your soul knows exactly how to heal itself. The challenge here lies in silencing the mind. Bring and soul and mind in unison until you feel a sense of calmness and peace.

Now, the violet light is gradually transforming into a beautiful green light. The anger has transformed into magical healing. The green light has completely surrounded you, healing every layer of your physical and metal self. The green light fades slowly. The screen has now gone blank. The lights are gradually turned on. The green light is passing through every heart cell, infusing it with forgiveness and healing. No region of your heart remains untouched by the magnificence of the green, healing light. You are awash with a profound feeling of peace, forgiveness and love. There is no absolutely no room for pain, guilt, hurt and regret.

You feel complete and immune to pain now. Results may vary from person to person. While some may move over their past quickly, others may require a few sessions to release pent up negative emotions. This can be practiced multiple times until you all your anger, guilt, pain and trauma has evaporated. Every ounce of anger should melt from your physical, mental and spiritual self before you stop this session.

Get ready to move your awareness back into the waking consciousness. Draw awareness to your body by breathing slowly and gently. Open your eyes slowly. You are now ready to take on the world with a renewed sense of forgiveness.

CHAPTER 7

The Twenty Minute Body Scan

Duration: 20 minutes

Objective: To experience a sense of calmness and gratitude.

The meditation is fundamentally important for killing fear, denial and awkwardness associated with developing familiarity with your body. It helps develop a deep sense of awareness, understanding and unconditional love for the body, simply for nourishing you and keeping you alive. Practitioners learn to explore the body"s fragility, tendency for injury and fragility. They learn to rise above pain and illness. You learn to cope with the eventuality of aging. Above all – there is a greater acceptance for what it is. There is a greater feeling of disenchantment yet complete compassion and peace with the physical body. There is a reduced tendency to become experience shock, distress or grief at getting injured, feeling hungry, growing old or becoming ill. By employing the body as study mechanism, practitioners learn to cope with the body's warning signals.

To set the record straight, beginners may not be able to instantly slip into a daily 15-minute meditation session. People fail to establish a 15 minute and half hour routine right at the onset of their practice, only to express disappointment for the practice altogether. "Oh! It didn't work for me." Meditation is not different from mastering any discipline. It involves taking baby steps, mastering one small goal at the time before you leap to bigger ones. Take baby steps by meditating for 5 minutes a day to begin with. Gradually increase the duration to 10-15 minutes daily.

Be consistent and disciplined about the practice. Try and reserve a fixed hour for your meditation practice each day. This will bring about a greater sense of consistency and routine to it. Once you keep practicing it, it will become an enjoyable habit, a happy addiction that's tough to discard. Okay, even if you don't enjoy it like as much as a deep dish pizza, you'll still no longer feel a sense of anticipation, compulsion or dread about going through the practice.

Pro Tip – if you aren"t following a guided audio or video meditation and are always worried sick about exceeding your meditation duration, set a timer on your phone. This way you do not have to keep wondering how the number of minutes still left to practice. Find a serene, low-lit place. Some folks may prefer a bright or naturally-lit space. It all depends on what soothes your senses, while elevating your spirit all the same.

To do a body scan meditation, be aware of various body parts such as arms, legs and torso. Mentally note the exact location of each of these bodily components. Start to divide them further into more intricate details. For instance, the arm can become the wrist, fingers, shoulder, elbow, palm and so on. Spend time on gaining awareness of
every part, including the sensations that are felt on it. Body awareness is not just about

gaining awareness but being completely aware of how each component feels, where exactly it is housed and what its true purpose is.

There are several other benefits of a body scan meditation. Several practitioners have found this technique to work wonderfully for pain management, boosted immunity, focused relaxation and greater physical responsiveness. You allow a compassionate, soothing and healing energy to pass into your being. There is a greater need to allow the body part to relax, repair and heal, which reduces stress and worry related issues.

What you are basically doing is a mental body CT scan. Have you ever seen CT scans? You can view your muscles, bones and internal organs. This is exactly what your mind is going to do in a body scan meditation. You may end up experiencing sensations or being completely aware of a particular body part.

Begin – Sit on a chair with overlapped hands. Sitting on the ground can be uncomfortable for many. Keep your back straight and head held up.

Shut your eyes slowly. Don"t do it all mechanically. Take time to slip into the position and gradually start closing your eyes.

Gently, start checking in with the body. Notice how your toes feel. Move on to other parts of the body, including the legs, belly, torso and head.

How do your legs feel? Are they still or is there some movement in them? What sensations are you currently experiencing in your legs? Keep your focus on your legs and blank out other body parts. How does the skin on your leg feel? Do you feel a potent force in your legs that carries your entire body? How do the toes that are touching the ground feel. What sensations do you experience in your feet? Tune in very closely to the physical sensations felt in your toes, feet and legs.

Bring complete awareness to your breathing. Breathe in and breathe out. Notice touching the floor and feeling a sense of touch when your feet make contact with the floor or a chair. Take time to experience and explore each section of your body. How does your body feel when you breathe in let in a gush of air into it? Experience the feeling closely. What sensation does the body feel when exhale a gush of air from the body.

Move to any region of your choice. Where exactly is it located in the body? What is its purpose within the cycle of your bodily functions? How did it originate? What does it need to sustain? Examine the experiences of the mind. How does the mind complement the body? For instance, when the mind experiences stress, the heart rate changes and muscles feel tense. Practice breathing in and out intentionally. You may do a complete body scan starting from the head and going right up to the feet. Sensations can also be explored or investigated randomly.

Your experiences can include a tingling sensation, temperature, pressure or just about anything that is noticed. Sometimes, you may not feel anything at all. Things may just be neutral. That is alright too. Notice these neutral feelings nevertheless. There"s no good and bad, no wrong or right. Simply tune in to the present without judgment. It"ll change the way you start perceiving things. Keep your mind open, curious and compassionate to whatever sensations you are exploring.

Now, release focus from whichever region, you were concentrating on and move to explore another part.

At some point you may start thinking about the last Game of Thrones you watched, and find your focus wandering. Wonderful! It simply means that you are noticing your mind straying. You"ll know quickly into the practice that the mind cannot help wandering. However, over a period of time, it will be trained to be still for a longer duration. The idea is to gently and compassionately train it and not force it. Draw attention to exploring your bodily sensations. Neuroscience has pointed to the fact that simply noticing our wandering attention and then bringing it back gradually and gently to our object/thought/area of focus creates new brain pathways.

Try and think about your personal experiences of the mindbody interaction. How does the body actually feel when there is an underlying fear, stress, uneasiness and tension? When the mind is calm, soothing and relaxed, how exactly does your body feel? When the mind is completely relaxed, doesn't the body feel exceedingly relaxed as well?

Is there any sense of attachment or wish that occurs in connection with a body part? What feelings are experienced by the mind when you spot something really beautiful and positive?

When you graduate to the head, imagine a soothing white room. Focus on your mentally created room. There will some buzzing in your mind. Focus on it too. Sometimes, you will invariably find yourself concentrating on nothing, which is wonderful too. Your mind will be hijacked with thoughts about what's cooking for supper or a string urge to scratch your feet. These are natural.

Such moments will occur throughout your meditation practice, however long you"ve been practicing for. Simply let go of the distracting thought with patience, compassion and gentleness. Bring your focus back on those "nothingness" thoughts or the white room.

When you finish the exploratory body sensations scan, take a few minutes for expanding your realm of attention. Feel your body breathing without any restrictions. Slowly open your eyes.

Meditation is not about eliminating or discarding distracting thoughts. It is accepting that the mind wanders, as long as you can recognize when it happens and get yourself back to your focus. Now, open your eyes slowly and get back to the real world. Boost your capacity to draw complete attention on real time feelings and sensations involving nothing but the present.
Train the mind slowly to accept both the pleasant and not so

pleasant sensations. Learn to notice simply by being there and noticing what's going on in the body rather than feeling the urge to fix everything that causes discomfort.

Don't you experience a renewed sense of familiarity, acceptance and understanding with your physical faculties? Isn't there a greater sense of gratitude for the gifts you've been blessed with? Don't you feel blessed for the physical, mental and spiritual gifts you've been endowed with?

CHAPTER 8

The 25 Minute Blissful Mind Meditation

Duration: 25 Minutes

Objective – Attaining a blissful and relaxed state of being.

Ensure that you are wearing loose and comfortable clothing. Let your hands lie loosely on the lap.

Let"s begin.

Shut your eyes. Relax completely.

With shut eyes, start connecting with the world inside you. Be aware of your internal feelings and thoughts. Slowly, blank out the external world from your realm of awareness. Take a few minutes to give yourself the freedom to enjoy a soothing and relaxing experience. For a few minutes, you are completely liberated from all responsibilities. Discard thoughts of tasks that are waiting to be completed. If you catch your mind straying during the session, gently draw the awareness back to the sound that is guiding you towards complete relaxation, tranquility and stillness.

You are always in control. If you desire to stop the session, just open your eyes. Take a slow extended breath. Release your breath. Feel yourself relaxing completely.

Take an extended, deep and slow breath again. Release it.

Take another deep and intense breath. Exhale.

Simply notice the calmness in the breath. Become aware of a relaxed feeling that is beginning to engulf your entire body.

Continue breathing slowly, deeply, compassionately and gently.

Notice your thoughts becoming lighter. They are now gradually floating in the air. They are drifting in the air, slowly moving up into the universe. The thoughts are becoming lighter and lighter and making their way further up into the air. The thoughts have now drifted far away, yet are accessible when you want them to be. They haven"t left your conscious state permanently. The thoughts are only helping you attain a state of gentle bliss and relaxation.

Experience a profound spaciousness developing inside you. The space inside you is completely empty now.

Relax completely.

Let the gentle movement of the breath direct you into a completely relaxed state.

Breathe in and out. Go deeper into your being.

Again in and out. Let your mind gradually slow down.

Breathe in and out.

You are in a completely relaxed state now. It is now time to begin a guided journey into a place of tranquility and bliss.

Allow visuals to be created in your naturally.

If mental visuals are hard to come by, just enjoy a sensory experience of your dream surroundings than viewing them in the mind"s eye.

Release all expectations. Allow yourself to witness the guide journey in a natural and seamless manner.

Start imagining that you are on a lush and lovely grassy field.

Feel the sun"s warmth caressing your body and face.

The breeze is slowly making its way towards you.

Feel the soft, dew-drops filled grass under your naked feet. The moisture is gently kissing the tips of your toes.

Witness the haunting sounds of nature surrounding you.

Feel the hustling of the lush green tree"s soothing branches.

There"s a waterfall in the background, which is making a haunting and soothing gushing sound as it elegantly cascades. The sound of flowing water instills a sense of energy and calmness in your spirit. You feel a deep sense of harmony with nature. Nature is soothing you and energizing you all the same with its magnificence.

Become aware of a bird"s pleasant song slowly originating in the background. It gets louder with every breath you take.

Feel the sound of the wind blowing through your hair. It is touching your face and hair with its natural magnificence. It is moving from your face and hair to your shoulders, chest and belly. It gradually makes its way to your legs, feet and toes. The hustling wind symbolizes an indomitable spirit that tests your strength and offers you respite from the heat all the same.

You are home in the idyllic destination. A safe haven. This is the place you belong to. This is your space. This is where your mind, body and spirit experience and unmatched

sense of unison. You are free from stress, anxiety and nervousness here. There is no time to worry. You are filled with extreme positivity and elation.

You have a lot of time at hand. There is no rush to head anywhere or get anything done. This time is yours alone.

There is a deep feeling of safety and happiness.

There is not stress or anxiety touching you here. You are only living in a state of pure, undisturbed and unaffected bliss.

Take time out to appreciate the surroundings you live in.

Become aware of a big tree growing in the vicinity.

There are lots of birds happily chirping on the branches of this tree.

Begin walking towards the tree. Feel relaxed yet energized with every step you take towards the tree. Feel yourself going closer to the tree with each deep breath. You are now standing facing the magnificent, gigantic and marvelous creation of nature. Nature"s wonders never cease to amaze your spirit. You experience an incomparable feeling of communion with nature.

Take time to become completely aware of each moment and fully experience every step. Be aware of everything you do without judging it. If distracting thoughts make their way into the mind, be aware of them and gently put them aside to focus on the powerful imagery.

Feel yourself getting into a deep state of relaxation. You are slowly but surely reaching a state of blissful relaxation.

Stand beneath the tree. Feel its sturdy branches and huge leaves stand above your head. Experience a strong feeling of protection under its glorious shelter. Nature is a brilliant healer and protector. It alleviates our woes to help us slip into a state of positivity, elation and hopefulness. Experience your stress melting away slowly as you become one with nature.

The tree is completely enveloped with delicious and juicy fruits of various colors, shapes and sizes. This is isn"t an ordinary tree. Its fruits have extraordinary powers. Imagine its sweet, ripe and delicious fruits falling all around you.

Reach out and enjoy a fruit piece. Examine the fruit closely for some time. What is the color of the fruits? What is its weight, size and texture?

Take a big bite now. Experience the fruit filling up your mouth.

As the fruit enters your throat and stomach, an amazing thing happens.

A feeling of deep happiness starts to grow deep within you.

The sensation originates in the stomach and travels all the way to the heart, lungs and chest.

Release thinking. Focus on nothing else but the feeling. Cherish this sensation of well-being and gentle love. Feel your spirit light up.

Take another fruit bite. Savor its sweet, juicy and delicious taste.

The amazing feeling has grown even more intense now.

Feel yourself glowing with a strong sensation of happiness, well-being and love.

Take another bite of the wonder fruit. The big can be as big as you want. Eat as much as you can. Relish its sweet spirit.

Relax completely and let yourself be overcome with a delightful feeling. Do not force yourself to do it. Simply let it take over your spirit effortlessly. Let it grow as much as you wish it to. Let it cover your entire body. Let every cell within your body experience this feeling of delightfulness and bliss.

Now, visualize yourself on an idyllic beach. It is a warm, bright and sunny day. The weather isn"t too hot. There is a pleasant and light breeze. You are gradually feeling the warmth of the sun infusing energy into your skin. Hear the refreshing and gentle waves licking the sand. Enjoy your communion with nature. You are experiencing a complete sense of oneness with nature.

There is no one else on the lovely beach. Yet, you feel a complete sense of safety. There is no danger lurking around anywhere. You are in an absolutely safe, secure and private space. You remove your footwear and place them on the flowy, balmy and golden sand. Experience how the tiny sand particles feel against your feet. Imagine walking on the warm, invigorating and energy infusing sand. There is a low sound of seagulls prancing above the water. The sound is faint yet audible. It adds a deep sense of tranquility to the setting.

You are now beginning to walk towards the pristine water. Walk adjacent the shore, where the sand, rocks and water meet. The sand feels soft, calm and cool. There is a pleasant breeze blowing in the air. The air is pure, fresh and rejuvenating. Slowly, let the

tension in your body evaporate as you walk in the sand. With every step you take, the tension is decreasing. All your stress, worries and tensions are slowly fading away. There"s no room for anxiety here. It is all peace, calm and relaxation.

Take a deep breath and breathe out slowly. Take another intense breath and breathe out gradually and gently. Experience the life force elements of nature refilling your senses with calmness and energy. Visualize any region in your body that feels aches, tensions and pains. Now imagine this stress slowly passing away and being released from your body. As water flows to the shore, it washes away all your tiredness, stress and worries. It all flows away along with the water. You are now in an absolute state of serenity and idyllic peace on the beach.

Now, a strong wave comes gushing to the shore. You bend down slightly and spot a bottle neat your foot. Instinctively, you reach out to pick it up. The bottle is now in your hands. It is cork sealed with a message note held within it. You pull open the cork, and expectantly reach out for the paper held inside the bottle. Experience gradually unfolding the paper and reading everything that"s written in there.

"For whoever reads these words, understand that this message is to reach out to you and let you know how special your actually are. You are unique and eternally loved. I have picked you to receive love, and pass it around to other people and planet earth.

Help them heal. Never for a second doubt about how special you are or your power to change the world." – The Universe.

On the reading the words, you are elated beyond measure. There is a deep sense of being able to touch other lives, which is why you want several others to discover this message in a bottle. You neatly fold the piece of paper and place it in the bottle. The bottle is resealed. Now, you throw it back to where it came from so someone else can find it. The bottle has made its way into the ocean to inspire and touch some more lives along the way. The positivity chain has been carried forward. The good that was sent to you from the Universe and has been sent back to the Universe.

The Universe has just conveyed to you that you are special and loved. Now, slowly visualize an angel approaching towards you. The angel is carrying a huge box that is filled with jigsaw puzzle pieces. You are now asked to pick pieces of your choice in whichever color, shape and image you like right there on the beach. The pieces are all arranged on the sand. The angel slowly whispers into your ear that you are just about to put together a puzzle of your existence. It says this and slowly walks away from, fading into the horizon.

You now have the freedom to select any images you like and complete the puzzle of your life. Pick words, shapes, symbols and colors that bear a special significance in your life. Select images that are especially meaningful for you. Put the pieces together seamlessly as you create the ideal life picture. Take a few minutes to visualize the puzzle you"'ve created. How has this puzzle turned out? Reflect on your choices by spending a few reflective and peaceful moments.

It is slowly time to move out of the meditation. Start bringing your body into a state of awareness. Feel the glowing force take over your entire body. Start with the toes, move up the feet, ankles, legs, thighs, stomach, chest, shoulders, neck, face and head. The glow has now taken over your entire body. You are completely relaxed and in a state of bliss now. Slowly open your eyes. Take a few seconds to gather yourself and gain awareness of the waking consciousness. Get ready for a joyful and blissful day ahead or a calm, relaxed night ahead.

CHAPTER 9

The 30-Minute Meditation

Duration – 30 Minutes

Objective – Complete Relaxation of the Body, Mind and Spirit.

Sit in a comfortable posture. Relax completely to release any stress from your muscles. Sit upright and avoid slumping. The ideal would be a clam yet alert state. Maintain your regular attentive posture to prevent yourself from falling asleep. You can also simply lay down and meditate. Do what works best for you.

Let us begin the meditation session now.

Start by taking many deep breaths. Keep the focus on your stomach, and continue breathing. Let the mind relax. Forget your worries. Remember, you are now in a safe haven where nothing can stress you. Take deep, slow and intense breaths. Imagine air entering your belly.

We will now utilize the power of color energy to eliminate stress from the body. Visualize a serene green light circle taking shape right above your head. The energy circulates in waves and drips on you. It is everywhere now. The green waves are dripping all around you. They have encircled you. The light energy is moving gradually, changing into cocoons encircling the body. The green light energy is forming a protective and healing circle around you for as long as you are meditating. It starts from the head and goes right down to the feet.

Every time you inhale from the nose, you are drawing in green energy from the cocoon. Pull the green energy into the body, down to your belly. Feel the energy spreading through the body and eliminating stress as you breathe out. Imagine the energy spreading internally as you breathe. It is soothing and relaxing. The green energy circulates within the body. It pushes out negative energy with each breath out.

Visualize the breath and the energy flowing within. Hear the energy in motion as it makes sounds along with the tune of your breath. The energy soothes and relaxes your muscles. As green energy moves in the body, all the negative energy is pushed out with every breath out.

Imagine this energy gradually moving to your head, then slowly taking over the lungs and moving outwards. The energy is soothing the muscles it passes through. You can lead this powerful energy wherever you desire. You are simply borrowing from the vast reserves of energy that are encircling you and moving all around you.

Every time you borrow this energy within the body, you end up experiencing a greater feeling of relaxation and control. Feel this powerful energy on your face. Feel it

revitalizing and rejuvenating the muscles on the face. It is now loosening, soothing and relaxing all your muscles. Relax the forehead. Shut your eyes. Let the energy slowly move into your cheeks and finally take over the jaw. Feel all your muscle tension and stress melting away. Now exhale completely. Feel the facial muscle tension being released.

The energy is now completely moving through your breath, down to the neck. It circulates in a swirly pattern, encircling the complete neck region. The energy is doing nothing but easing your neck muscles, while letting you breathe more easily. The tightened muscles have been opened. They are now completely relaxed. Exhale to feel stress within the neck region melt away. It is slowly leaving your body.

Inhale deeply. Feel the energy taking over your shoulder and chest muscles now. The energy touches the muscles and completely de-stresses them. Your shoulders droop slightly and the chest stays still while you breathe deeply. Breathe gently by breathing in and out the belly. Keep the shoulders and chest completely relaxed now. Experience the energy taking over the chest and shoulder region, and releasing any pent up tension.

Fully relax your muscles. Breathe out and witness all your tensions fade away while breathing.

As you breathe in, witness the energy moving down to your arms. The energy takes over your arms, right down to every finger. The energy flows down your biceps and triceps, letting the muscles feel rejuvenated and relaxed. All the injuries and pain you've accumulated in the region through daily athletic or desk job activities are dwindling away. The energy is releasing pain and substituting it with a strong feeling of renewal.

Gradually relax your wrists. Take each finger at a time. Experience each finger being filled with a healing energy. As you exhale, the energy is passing through your arms, taking the pent up negative energy. It leaves your arms that toil hard throughout the day, feeling lighter, renewed and more stressfree.

Relax the stomach that has been letting this energy into the body. Let the flow of your breathe relax it and infuse it with even more energy. The muscles in motion are now completely relaxed, making the way for your internal organs to receive a soothing massage, which takes the relaxation process even further.

On the next breath, feel the energy flowing deeper into the stomach and taking over the entire pelvic region. The energy fills your hips and gently relaxes all muscles and organs held within the pelvic region. This supreme energy draws the region into a state of harmony. It releases pent up sexual tension. When you breathe out, the stress in your pelvic area and hips is released from the body, leaving a warm and refreshed feeling.

Now, you will suck the energy deep into your legs to fill up your leg muscles. Think about the legs that hold the weight of your body. They help you move around through

the day. Can you imagine the build-up of stress and tension? It will all be released soon. Breathe deeply. Every breathe fills your legs with energy, starting with the thighs, and gradually move downwards. As the energy passes through your legs, allow the muscles to ease up. Your thighs are now completely limp with zero stress residing in there.

The energy is gradually moving through your knees, soothing any pain and injuries with a replenished healing sensation. The energy is dripping down your calf muscles. It is flowing to your shins. The energy brings all your tension and stress to the ground. All the stress is evaporating through your feet. Feel the energy slowly moving up the ankle now. The energy begins to take over your feet. Experience the muscles within your feet relax completely. The energy spills into every toe and slowly moves towards the feel pads. Feel it relaxing the heels. The energy is actively working towards releasing all the pain and tension housed in the region by walking.

When you breathe out, green energy is released through the feet, getting back to its original cocoon. All your body tension, stress and pain evaporate with this green energy. The body is now encircled by a rejuvenated circle of energizing, calming and healing energy. With every breath you take, your body is filled with a deep sense of healing and calmness. Continue to heal, soothe your senses and relax as we continue.

We will continue the meditation by slipping into a deeper state of relaxation and bliss. As you enter a deeper meditation state, you are absolutely in control of your being and the energy that transverses through your being. Even from inside, the energy remains with you, offering you a more positive, healing and rejuvenating protection.

Now that you are completely relaxed, forget about the body. Allow the consciousness to be directed solely on your inner world. Move inwards. Allow the imagery to uncover from within your inner self. Visualize yourself being protected by the energy cocoon. You are now safely seeing everything unfolding before you in the powerful mind"s eye.

A circular white halo of energy suddenly starts to take shape below you. This is only but a means of taking you into a more intense state of consciousness. It will transport you into a universe of absolute peace. Imagine an elevator gradually lifting you into a deeper state of consciousness. You have complete control of the elevator as you breathe.

When you breathe in, the white energy ring sparkles and takes life, getting ready to take you into deeper mental levels. While breathing out, the elevator slowly lowers down. Experience the floor under you taking slow yet firm motions. There"s absolutely no danger. You are in a protected and secure personal zone that has been created only by you. Tune into the soothing humming sound of the elevator. Now you see the numerical 1 just above the head. Under the numerical 1 is the word Relax, glowing in a bright blue neon shade.

Breathe in deep into the belly. Let the green energy completely soak your body. Move slightly lower mentally. Stay aware, calm and alert nevertheless. When you breathe out, you move through number 2 just over the head. Again, the word Relax sparkles just below number 2 is bright neon blue. Once you see the incandescent word, you feel a deeper sense of relaxation and comfort. The glowing light keeps humming as one moves deeper. You are heading to a solid, powerful and secure place. Inhale now. Keep increasing the green energy housed within you. Mentally, move lower now. Breathe out. Release negative energy. Witness the numerical 3, along with Relax. Relax is getting larger and more prominent with each subsequent level.

Let the subsequent inhalation take you lower. You are now into a state that is deeper than you"ve experienced in the session. The green energy is now more intense than you"ve ever witnessed. It is held with the protective circle. It can be found flowing and moving around freely, while still being with you. The energy is gradually growing within you as you take slow, deep breaths. All the negative energy is slowly being pushed out. You exhale and view number 4 just above the head. There is the Relax word again, becoming even more defined and larger than before.

You are now located halfway there. All your negative energy has been kept behind. As you breathe in and move deeper, the energy increases within you. You are completely soaked with this profound, intense, powerful and positive energy. All the negative energy has been released and left behind at the previous level.

Breathing out completely, you go through level 5, and spot Relax just above it. It is now conspicuous and clearly visible in the mind"s eye. There"s no difficulty in viewing it. Even if you cannot spot the word, feel its vibrations. Hear it being played out several times in the head. Hear the word Relax gaining strength and guiding you every step of the way.

Take a few deep breaths. You are heading into a more intense state of relaxation. All the accumulated negativity has been abandoned. Focus on letting it all go. Release all your tensions, stress and worries. Nothing will bother you now. You are in a safe, stress-free and serene space. Nothing will affect you here. Any sounds you catch now will make the process of slipping into your space even deeper. The noises are distant. Nothing can distract your or take away from your concentration.

Take a long, deep breath into your belly. Extend the stomach outwards. The chest feels more relaxed. The air passes deeper into the lungs effortlessly. Take a deep breath now. Move lower. Breathe out deeply. You now see spot number 6 and feel the term Relax on your body. It has enveloped your entire body. It can be spotted and heard, becoming more and more intense, while helping you.

Take a pleasant and intense breath. Gradually, move into a deeper state. When you breathe out, number 7 is shinning bright right above your head. The word Relax is now reverberating through your being. It is there everywhere in your body. Each body cell has been covered by its sheen. Simply hear it and feel it moving through your body.

Practice deep breathing. Take slow, deep and intense breaths to move to the next level. You are completely relaxed now, and are now fully within the mind. There is absolutely no sound from the external world. The physical body is well-protected in its current restful position.

You are in a gently relaxed yet alert position. A powerful and formidable calm is now a part of your being. Breathe out and go past number 8, witnessing it just above your head. The word Relax is now fully immersed into you. It is being gently repeated and communicated to the subconscious.

Take another deep breath. Move into a deeper level of the mind. Relax gently. Breathe out and go past number 9. Do not do anything more. Stay calm. Do not react or make anything. Each thing is being passively created with absolute ease and clarity.

Breathe in slowly, gently and deeply, moving into the deepest consciousness levels that you've witnessed. You are filled with relaxation, healing power and energy, which can be monitored. Feel it in motion. It is taking away all your problems. Witness your body being healed. You are feeling instantly younger. There is a feeling of being renewed, balanced and alive. When you breathe out, the numerical 10 is right over your head. You have completely arrived. There is a deep sense of arrival within your personal space of rejuvenation, relaxation and power. It is time to reveal your glorious, true self.

The door to your personal space is filled with power. It can be anything you want it to be. It takes shape inside your mind. Borrow from childhood memories, when you were completely at ease. There was control, innocence and vision. Now, you get to mould that vision. Look out into the world. Watch natural wonders such as the mountains and beaches take shape right before you.

As you get ready to move into your powerful personal space, the door is slowly sliding back. It exposes a slight trace of sunlight, while beginning to move away. Imagine a stunningly breathtaking landscape. A tranquil river is flowing under the elevator. It slowly trickles and transverses rocky river beds. It travels into a spectacular landscape of lush and nourishing trees.

Step out gently. Feel the cool, soothing water on your naked feet. The rocks feel smooth, serene and grounded. They are firm. There"s no way for you to slip.

You are completely at peace within your personal space of power. There is no care in the world. You can be whatever you fancy. For some time, feel the water licking your feet. It is constantly moving, carrying your thoughts along. Walk through the lush grass and experience its serenity on your toes and feet pads. You are now relaxing under the shade of a large tree. There is a large clearing that is a perfect setting to relax under the scintillating light of the sun. The sun"s rays can be seen cutting through the trees" branches. The sun"s soothing and gentle rays warmly caress your skin. Clouds are

passing by leisurely, offering you a cool respite. Stay here for a few seconds. Experience a sense of communion with nature. Stop thinking or worrying about the external world.

Your mental state is now restored. It gets this profound feeling that it is where it belongs. It belongs to you. The mind is now one with the body. Carry this sense of oneness all through the day. The powerful personal space is available when it is needed. It can be when you need it the most. Nothing has the ability to cause you harm when you reside in this powerful personal space. No one can enter your personal space

Powerful when you don"t want to let them in. You can get back whenever you want. You are now ready to take care of your loved ones.

Now gently move away from the river, and move to the elevator. It attempts to take you back to your individual pace. Gradually, each breath draws into a sense of waking awareness. The elevator door slides behind. You are now embarking this journey at the bottommost level. You can spot a pure, white energy surrounding you. The energy, serenity and tranquility are intact.

The energy starts buzzing and surrounds you. You are now able to clearly see the numerical 10 light up over your head. Inhale deeply. Exhale while inching closer to awareness or consciousness. Now, gradually the numerical 9 appears above the head. You feel a greater sense of alertness. You are completely awake now. As you breathe out, you are inching more and more towards waking consciousness and awareness.

You can now slowly spot the numerical 8 just over the head. It has a faint blue inscribed under it. The word is "awake" is written right under the number 8. As you breathe out, you pass the words, going even further. Now you see number 7, and the word, "alert" shining brightly. The soothing blue light emitted by the words brings you greater awareness and focus. Breathe out and slowly move towards a sense of waking awareness.

As you breathe in, spot number 6 right over your head with the words, "awake" written below it. The green light energy around you is gradually turning into a soothing blue. It energizes your mind, body and spirit. Feel it relaxing you and getting the mind into absolute focus.

Breathe in intensely. Draw in the cool blue energy into your belly. The energy is now moving throughout the body. The numerical 5 is now prominently visible over the head. The word, "awake" is getting larger gradually. It is more prominent and defined. It is being repeated in the mind. Feel the vibrations buzzing around throughout your being. Breathe out and feel a sense of transporting into a higher sense of stillness, passing the number.

Breathe completely into the belly, throwing more soothing blue energy into your body. The energy is passing through the head right now. You are completely soaked into its relaxing, serene and soothing effects. The number 4 is now visible over your head, with the word "awake" written under it. It draws you into a greater sense of alertness and

focus reverberating through your body. Now breathe out. Traverse through the number and words into a fully awakened state.

Breathe into the belly using the regular belly breathing method. Soak the soothing blue energy all through your body. Feel a sense of invigoration and stillness. Number 3 is lighting up above you. See the word "alert" just below it. Begin to feel the emotion of alertness and awareness throughout your body. Let the sensation occupy your mind. Sit peacefully. You have chosen to move into a highly alert and awakened breathing state.

Breathe in now with a highly awakened focus. Gradually and faintly, you are able to spot the numerical 2 under the head. You are now resting in a completely conscious and alert state yet opt for stay in the personal cocoon, absorbing every ounce of energy into the body. The word "awake" is now circulating all through the body. The mind is occupied by it too. You have chosen to let this energy fill up your physical and mental faculties. They are conspicuously defined. You feel a natural sense of elation and energy to hear the vibrations of these words with each cell of your body. If infuses you with a sense of joy, calmness, relaxation and positivity. Exhale slowly now into a state of waking consciousness. Carry serenity, energy and relaxation within your senses.

When you inhale, the energy is brought under full control. It brings a sense of mental clarity and energized actions. You are now very slow to witnessing numerical 1, with the term "awake", which has totally engulfed you now. It is deep inside you. Slowly open your eyes. Breathe out. All your worries, stress, tension and anxieties have evaporated. Your mind is completely focused and you are now in absolute control and in a heightened state of being. The energy that has been carried along with you is circulating with the body, bringing you an incomparable sense of calmness and focus all through the day. Recall for a single moment, the jubilation and extreme happiness that has claimed your personal powerful space.

Utilize this blissful feeling to remind yourself all through the day that no one other than you is in control of your life and actions. The feeling will quickly dawn upon you during challenging times. It is a vital part of your being now. The feeling is your second skin. The feeling cannot be forgotten or castaway. It has become a vital component of you.

You are now feeling absolutely relaxed, blissful, focused and prepared to take on the world. Take a moment to lie still and enjoy this blissful feeling. Know that you can draw from it whenever required. Lastly, do not forget to keep a smiling face throughout the day. Enjoy yourself. Enjoy a pleasant, invigorating and refreshing day.

CONCLUSION

Thank you for downloading this amazing book.

I sincerely hope it was successful in helping you fulfill your goal of achieving happiness, positivity and relaxation through meditation.

The next step is to practice the various meditation techniques mentioned in the book, for simply reading about these techniques without applying them is sheer wasted opportunity. The various meditation sessions are packed with clear and simple instructions to get you started with your practice right away. So, do not hesitate to begin using these methods to slip into a dedicated and consistent meditation practice.

Lastly, if you truly enjoyed the book, please take time out to share your thoughts and post a review on Amazon. It''d be highly appreciated!

www.ingramcontent.com/pod-product-compliance
Lightning Source LLC
Chambersburg PA
CBHW071502070526
44578CB00001B/415